As Much As

ALLAN PETERSON

salmonpoetry

Published in 2011 by
Salmon Poetry
Cliffs of Moher, County Clare, Ireland
Website: www.salmonpoetry.com
Email: info@salmonpoetry.com

ISBN 978-1-907056-58-1

Cover design: *Mike Manoogian, incorporating a drawing by the author*
Typesetting: *Siobhán Hutson*

We do what we can, we Muses

Frances Dunham

Acknowledgements

Grateful acknowledgements to the editors of the following journals and anthologies in which these poems first appeared:

42 Opus: "The Future We Can Name,"
Bayou: "Pure Description"
Beloit Poetry Journal: "As If Galvanic"
Blackbird: "Meanwhile," "Whim of the Minute"
Cordite (Australia): "The Rabbit Soprano"
ForPoetry: "There I Go Again," "Temporality"
Good Foot: "Perhaps"
Green Mountains Review: "Friday Driving Home," "Pillow of Stones"
Kennesaw Review: "Distraction"
Meeting of the Minds Journal: "Last Accomplishment"
Other Voices International: "Touch and Go"
Quercus Review: "So Taken"
Red Booth: "The Speed Of Light"
Small Spiral Notebook: "Excuses"
Square Lake: "An Irony"
Stickman Review: "No Gods Needed"
Story South: "As Much As," "The Small Gods," "Hurricane in Halves"
The Adirondack Review: "The Uses of Nature"
The Curbside Review: "Anxiety Dining"
The Gettysburg Review: "Given This," "Death About Love"
The King's English: "Anatomy and Clouds"
The Massachusetts Review: "Ago"
The Pedestal: "Making Sense"
The Seventh Quarry (Wales): "Cover"
Talking River Review: "Wrong Number"
Verdad: "Lyric"
West Wind Review: "Sleeves Ringing"

*Some of these poems may appear here
in slightly different form*

Contents

As Much As

Distraction

No Gods Needed

Under Orion

As Much As

AS MUCH AS

I have taken my chair into the undergrowth.
I sit above the dog long gone.
Around me an oval unfolds, the arcs of my vision
like the simplified maps
of the Middle Ages relying on Scripture,
not on looking for detail,
a world in a circle with no moving parts.
But this is not simple.
It would take days of naming to begin
to announce my visitors,
seeing within seeing like Hooke or Leeuwenhoek.
Said this way with exuberance,
it may fail to resemble any place you know.
But that is the way of attention;
it brings more than expected. And so before me
is the hot and moist, the four
elements and then some. The azalea as the answer
to iodine while spider silks tell the wind
better than the nylon sock or brass chicken on a rod.
And what looked alive was alive, and alive
within alive, and alive within that.
As far as I know. As I can see.
As far back as I remember. As much as I can stand.

SO TAKEN

The hours are so taken with themselves
planning what their gathered minutes will contain,
and the beach peas are so busy
portraying the ocean because they live by it
though their translation of swells into petals is imperfect,
spending time to devise keeled flowers
as lifeboats to save themselves,
and the present is so beside itself, stuttering
into something almost tangible that takes up space.
like writing a new love's name all over your notebooks—
the only instance of making a word more solid
by repeating, when ordinarily it dissolves—
clinging expectantly to the surprising irregularities
as door glass holds houseflies.

THERE I GO AGAIN

Small birds are wisdom while the large are hunger.
No, that is another theory altogether.
No one could answer for all those restless apartments,
for the nests like axioms in the window angles,
as if mathematics was certain as a sparrow's brown eyes,
the globe of an orange remembered from its peels.
Another is the reason the covers of my books curl volutes
like exquisite pleasures there on the deck rail courting sun,
or that tissue enflamed is first itself with no explanation
until something in the wild riot of the blood decides
on erection or fever. There I go again. I am like the ants
scrambling, unable to find the boot that ruined their nursery.
My guesswork is passing as purpose that satisfies worry.
Why the chickadees bathe in the drip plates.
Why a man must wear arrows while chained.

ANATOMY AND CLOUDS

I can wake up any morning
and there might be a sloop tied to the island
painted so white
I need to sweep the horizon to be sure
it's not a cloud
or I can yaw with it and see Connecticut the Keys
Frances I haven't taken my eyes from
Or stars might appear in my fingerprints
instead of whorls
or arcs or left loops the ordered streets of Harlem
and I wake to write about anatomy and clouds
using her measurements

TEMPORALITY

I cannot remember when the planet was pink at night.
I cannot recall a time when someone did not think
there were lines on the globe resembling a cage
with parallels as the arcs of circles and a fleet of caravels
protected by woodcuts.
I am looking at an acre of doily spiders betrayed by dew.
I am listening to music of such poignancy it should be
called a sympathy rather than symphony.
Because of the myth of immortality and the cloying cards,
I turned away. I forgot for a moment what I intended.
I turned like birds, like a knife in the light, and disappeared.

HURRICANE IN HALVES

By the time half the hurricane had passed, nine candles
had pooled in their saucers,
the cypress split in two above the Toyota. Before they extinguished
I could barely read Robert Graves,
and in the diminishing flicker "groves" became "gloves"
and the Caslon wavered on the page.
So in my reading it appeared the sacred gloves had closed around oxygen,
had twisted the weather till the cypress split lengthwise.
In the other six hours the Romantic was carried upstairs
with the clothes and photos.
Birds blown from their nests were dizzy trying to recover,
our once local insects were entering Atlanta.
So maybe the Big Bang was believable after all, maybe an axiom
might be married to a stove, pitchfork to pine sap,
any stair might be cousin to a ladder and the wormhole near the sill
emerge near Aldebaran in Taurus.

THE SMALL GODS

It is sometimes only a matter of mentioning the jewels,
the mockingbird's gold eye, the toad's,
the skins beaded and gem-cut like goannas and pangolins,
and especially diamondbacks.
Isn't that what we're talking about, how the simplest glitters
like treasure, like a crown,
how the innocent holds a key to what we call paradise
which is not exotic, but so ordinary
we miss it encrusted on a leaf or stuck to the sidewalk.
Here even the small gods get a chance,
and when I found one I called to Frances in sequins,
well, rain drops, to watch the cicada,
or she calls me to the owl in the red cedar, the two shoes
eyeing each other by the bed,
the weave glistening heavenly out of plain materials.

FRIDAY DRIVING HOME

Slow motion is a dream for something our size.
The closest we have are afternoons,
hot Augusts just before a storm when the ponderous
cloud front approaches at a planetary pace.
Or like Friday driving home, a minute spider,
a thinking speck, arrived from nowhere and began
a web from my nail to my thumb knuckle.
And the massive traffic slowed, rattles dampened,
the bay bridge lengthened itself, and I began
to believe in the exquisite silhouette
more than the languid shadow, in the expansive power
of one inch, the uncial I shrank to
while the minuscule drama opened like a net,
the picture built between heartbeats,
a lace from Bruges that maps oceans from here to Polynesia.

GIVEN THIS

Leaf, whether gold or hickory, glitters like Las Vegas.
Foil, whether beaten sheet or a hastened plan thwarted,
gleams as if fresh from the photographer's sinks,
and anvils of vapor rise above the island like distractions.
While I am observing my veins, saying blood is delivered
faster right-handed because of the limb size, I find a bird hip
right on the sidewalk, and I am surrounded by an instant
mental fence of crime scene ribbons. I stand as a zero between
the unlikely and the taken on faith, and I wonder given this,
whether desert bees had indeed built a hive in the husk of a lion,
whether it was likely that anyone noticed how frequently
it was emptied of shining flesh, sweetness, and numerals.

DOCUMENTATION

Holbein had already resewn tapestries with paint,
Whistler rebuilt satin and ceramics,
and the microscopic oars of heliozoans
had sent their galleys like Xerxes into the Hellespont
in the slide of pondwater,
not for battle, but threatening glitter and amazement.
Then I cramped my serratus,
a tightness I'd forgotten like chrome bumpers.
Then "cowhorse" appeared in someone's speech
as if it was not a paradox
confiscated for another purpose.
And here comes Holbein, bringing portraits to the king
from Amsterdam, as Montezuma
sent draftsmen to render the invading men of metal
and startling horses of Cortez.
Elsewhere depictions on a polished tooth, maps on a scapula,
truths recreated the size of a tick or birdseed.

WRONG NUMBER

They are within hearing but unheard
even when you hold them to your ear
the way people will touch a photo
in a private ritual. We answer.
There is an absent voice in the middle of static.
There is news we are not getting
even from those who may think us a restaurant
but one number off. Or maybe they know
and it's just reservations. Someone hungry to talk.
If they might just lean out their voices
this could be the call they want after all.
It could be the unexpected answer
like the chair that lifts you up when you can't.
It could be what they need before dinner.
We might say appetizer. Might say news like a protein.
Might say everything that can be made
special in the dark with an egg and green leaves.

BAD NEWS FAST

Long stalks drowsy, short ones nervous.
We were agitated like someone mowed around us
left us standing for some special attention
while the sky toppled over. And that's not all.
Its surprising weight had us worried.
Silver birds had stayed on their halves and quarters
unless thumbed to invisibly for luck.
The mail planes stayed grounded on their stamps
while absinthe in the form of a lime-clouded storm
was headed down our throats and up
through the sandy shallows to the fogged-in moon.
That's when I heard the bad news fast that spread
accurate as bats led by their echoes. Even the flies
stopped rubbing their hands in satisfaction.

COVER

Cheetahs, all periods and tear-stained faces,
figure for themselves
how long it takes to go from grasses to a spotted cat,
how to speculate safely from cover
on the sister-filled universe of burst hearts and trampled flowers
Nearby a river slows
by banking to see the tips of the garden burn
flowers and bearded cereals,
grasses concealing one life against another, fringes of sky,
acres of uncles
unkempt, torturing daisies for love me's
Sometimes I look at the landscape the way our spaniel stared
at the wall like an idiom,
a meadow of stickpins and seeded fields hiding lovers
whose eyes glow red in the distance

Distraction

DISTRACTION

We want to read and sing at the same time
We want to say no place lacks bacteria and be sure
We want to believe time
was altered by our presence that martinis
and opium harbor gods
We do not want to hear "returned to normal"
Normal contained us
We want that edge with an exit
We want to say rhyme or reason as if
that meant a consequence
connected with another world as fallback
We want to remember
in the beginning distances were so vast
nothing had voices but needed translation
and poetry began where we stepped in to listen
and notice repeatedly stars
were a belt and sword and contained a galaxy
We were just getting comfortable
when the signer misspelled sygyzy
but who could blame her
what with everyone staring at the stars
rubbing dangerously together on her dress

AGO

Plentiful decorations with no trace,
hot trees and vessels of the mesenteric
as far back as motion set apart by rhythms
of the day/night breath,
remindful heart and fluids of the nearby
wordless villages.
Lushness starts it, not a bland abstraction
that goes back to a single something,
one worm in a tight spot containing a universe.
No, that is a poor science.
A bare room anywhere comes with nostalgia,
the slightest mention
of a glance's wistful irretrievability.
The worst is having the familiar turn on you,
the black lab in the dream that bit me,
tonight a cheetah,
something once trustworthy in the dust
that lived quietly with a hidden and malevolent purpose,
a loved thing with intent never suspected,
less than sulfur, less than the silicate minerals,
or the wren that built a surprising womb of twigs
in the mailbox.

SPIRAL STRESSES

They are open, the silk and wire flowers,
resin for dew,
copper *Vanessa* on a stalk twirling *ersatz*
in the cobalt bowl
because the others needing water
will not sit still,
stop unfolding. I love
how my veins have found their way
down my forearm
to my hands, yours in roughly the same way:
riverine, sanguine, serpentine.
I sit here while you are a shadow on the moon
from my smiling,
and all the entries in the index are parts of speech
though heavy on the nouns.
The articles often overused for emphasis are creating
their own gravity,
begin to turn around an emerging center, a stamen,
a nexus, a fly attending a blue flag iris.

THE FUTURE WE CAN NAME

Nothing is motionless, not the painted portrait
blinking while you're away,
whose acids are discoloring buttons, whose frame
is oxidizing while moistening its eyes,
or the uneasy sky pieced together from brushstrokes.
We stand on the deck with bread crumbs.
Seagulls appear in the air before us. This story
will spread like salamanders
born from the mating of fire and dead logs.
Each day we could have died we woke up
grateful after so many accidents,
tensions of things trying not to be their progenitors,
not determined by the heartworms of destiny.
The future we can name is the one hoped for,
duplicating yesterday's sex. The real one
is unpredictable as when the final original flake
of The Last Supper will loosen and fall,
the restorations and postcards taking over,
every day having its teeth hidden by its grin.

EXCUSES

They speak them, the crows,
night-shatters with complaints: why they didn't reintegrate
how they couldn't be other
than left over, or be the embroideries of hallucinations in daylight.
They had been lighting up the faces of skeptics
with their listing of predicaments and singleness of purpose,
had been watching a tern mother
bring to her baby a minnow too big, so they stole it,
had been covering the roof of the clinic
till the AC startled them and the sky went dominos.
The adornment of poems required them,
they said, standing in for death and despicable wants,
tailored as they were for anxiety in dark suits,
mocking clerics, lying through their teeth.

DEATH ABOUT LOVE

It is a style —the boots that demonstrate
how ankles collapse—
as now that of the orphans whose fingers barely reach
beyond their sweaters,
the patient's lost hair, fur, the backwards hat.
We have skin, so it is unnecessary
to wear that of another.
It would show we were lying about compassion, death,
about love, about the oils of anointing
delivered by a dove for Clovis of the Franks,
or an angel to the kings of England.
So they are messengers, and the knot above the foot
speaks to destiny and sprains,
travel with a body, the body that dries out
and crumples like a shoe.

PURE DESCRIPTION

If it were dry, knives would stay sharp longer,
hitches stop slippage,
the arid idea of permanence would seem more deeply intended
and almost believable.
There would be no death birds unlaying in the air,
no serpents in clover.
But this is Florida, whose mornings are wet wings, whose
noons glisten and cannot be trusted.
Wear is the process of use and ruin but is also the polish
from touch to metals,
kisses to soapstone, handling brass and mahogany.
Tear is torn but healed by evening,
while tears are fluids affecting the elasticity of moments.
In the southern tradition
these are woven, and may require a spindle eye or splice,
if too much is asked of them.
We consult the table of breaking strengths. We generalize wildly,
hempen or wire.

PERHAPS

When we say the heart, we don't mean
what strums the bed springs.
When we say heaven,
we mean more than the prolonged emptiness
the rockets keep describing.
We are choosing things to blame:
the curved oceans clinging to nickel, a few lives,
geographies of the deep sea,
stairs that rise only to crash against the house.
We mean a thing almost transparent in passion,
sometimes starting with a hot soup
stirred by lightning and full of alphabets, sometimes
a garden before slugs and fire ants.
Sometimes we just fold red paper, and with scissors
cut a chain of shapes.

THE USES OF NATURE

It could have been dawn splintered by the sill
or some bright planks of yesterday
painted but forgotten and leaned against the wall
But I do not pretend an afterlife
not even for qualities That is why it is so poignant
what you do with this one
Almost no one is born at home light or day
and no one is less mysterious
At the festival yesterday a woman sold beadwork
She made ticks and mice
and scorpions a platypus a flea
She said for a child the heart moves over
and you begin to think of mint and unusual animals
No one is making these rats
This one is nothing you would know of she says
like people in paintings
that pretend living pretend movement
Do you have the dog that eats the moon a missile
No those are things men want
things brutal and useless But we are the women
We string secrets

SÉANCE

The way someone says "centerpiece"
and some think fat candles
surrounded by arrangements of berries
and ribbons and waxed leaves,
and others of the heart fully arborized
and spread beautifully
throughout the plexus and appendages
by the completeness of arithmetic and roses,
open like the wings of an altar from Siena,
a boy who died and was surrounded
by the foliage of grief,
like the enraptured consolation of literature,
like the young bronze couple
cast in the candelabrum herding their metal sheep
soundlessly on the small marble hillside,
the ants that have brought up ochres from below
and stacked them till they fell
into the recognizable the way someone wanting
to visit the dead must make a bell
of the planetary metals and visit the trailer
of Madame Lydia, reader and advisor on highway 98,
bring a book, a finger through a ring, twenty dollars
and the presence they paid for
would flit from sofa to vase or stand behind them
as ghostly as italicized lines.

NO URANIUM

As if time moved slower by the fire extinguisher
than by the phone
As if "right now" could be held in your hand
and examined
like the plain-faced decorations on a cup
spoken to reasoned with
As if all of this was history labored on a page
the gold leaf hours illuminations skin
by someone up early with no obligation
but to say this is thinking see how exquisite
And then the gold alone
quietly reflecting the grief of phenomena ecstasy
as if visiting Montana
believing the fiction of pure water air
filtered of particulates
No uranium no wondering nothing but chasing
what doesn't come to you
ignoring what does like being attracted and repelled
like breathing tides
where only the frequency changes as if writing
what might be said
but only to the paper notebook the phosphored screen

PILLOW OF STONES

Down to earth down
to magnolias dropping grenades red-eyed
up all night
Down to storms oppressing the open windows
down to the smallest historian
appearing to help us
to show up in culture with contrite conclusions
Down to a figure on a pillow of stones
a burial with a necklace of dentalia
dust in his eyes
As if plain bones were not enough
there is a skull cracked for emphasis
saying yes to the future
I was lucky I was not captured I was also
in your sad state
I had these few bowls and those
who propped me up
We are by now plentiful and useless
Look at Tikal
Sometime the sea will lessen
and there will be cliffs like Dover
carbon will tell you how heartless we were

SOMETHING IMPORTANT

Whose heels light up with each step
from pressure of the *avenidas*
going one way, *calles* the other,
laces where they cross,
have steps like soft coughs coming
from next door.
It is to be expected that in explanations
speed will fit into the metaphors
along with footbones and names of shore birds
for what they do—turnstone, skimmer,
and the way I think of your body beside me
like a hurdler in love and lofting backwards
arching over a bar, things linking up
by themselves, a pattern sewing Paraguay to stars
enough to give you the idea
something important is happening and something
important could be said in something
fragile as a poem about the capability of blood
and running as the joggers are joined
by bicycles with little reflectors on the spokes
so the lighted heels and eccentric spinning
join the moving stars and the fixed stars,
some in Orion, some along the driveway.

AN IRONY

Cats were climbing to the nest of woodpeckers
so I built a wide halo of wire.
I waited securely as if the First Principle was iron.
I watched the showers of yellow leaves
which are springtime in the South, then the owl
ate the babies instead. I forgot the agency of air
while reading that Hippo thought the First Principle water.
Now the texts I am attempting to reconcile
are those of the back yard to our skins and protections.
Necessity is the same as fate, says Leucippus.
Good to the last drop, says Maxwell.

No Gods Needed

NO GODS NEEDED

Saying bird is too big
     saying swallow is
Saying syrinx and all songs gathered in the throat
Saying those
who had globes were privileged those
on metal stands or those in the libraries
whose bearings were silent in their walnut carriages
     But I had a world map
that covered my wall above the painted radiator
Like a bird aloft I could see everything at once
     So no gods, no saints, just finches
No intercession, no afterlife,
     no souls smoking from the body,
no expectation but a dream
While I water
I see them visit the feeder So no gods needed,
     no explanations
It is enough to know they are finches,
and gold, and crave thistles

LYRIC

Something's got the Mergansers going:
        an opera The chorus
diving and flapping like flightless maniacs
        Reminds me of a song:
If whiskey was a river and I was a diving duck
as if to say simplify enjoy
throw up your hands to the waitress
        Dive Dive

A semaphore has three choices
        in infantile colors
Hold up the avenue is one Green is vanish
like slugged shots
        Now the fishermen in slickers poling home
with the dead engine
pause to ask if I have an oar they could borrow
They move off singing caution
        pass the flask It's dark at the bottom
and caked with weeds

MAKING SENSE

It was a song I loved but I skipped singing
and went down where beach peas wired up the pines
      and sharp-shins came for the catbirds.
New smilax had not yet hardened their horns
and were so many tomato worms.
Docks along the coast looked like a thumb piano.
      I listened.

We drink to the future. We eat to it. We have no choice
      chained together by hunger and expectation.
There on *Solidago* is a Red Admiral —another *Vanessa*—
whose worm I know and its host —nettles—
and the grey fox stepping away from the buckeye
      lemons ecstatic with sour
two end days rafted to a week. There is no "making sense,"
      it is sense already.

ANXIETY DINING

It was so threatening we lied to the knives
pointing them elsewhere
soup spoons already arched like an ecstasy
or tetanus
        lied to the salt
to the stitched and initialed lap cloths
to the invitations gilt-edged and pointed
like the forks
        Seating was arranged to meet proteins
guanine facing taurine and the rest in order
We could do nothing but drink and gossip
        uncertainty was thumping the fan itself
heartsick above the house
        The smiling wine
its blood-colored wavelengths
        one chipped star on the lip of each goblet
our slightest breath fear among candles

AS IF GALVANIC

As soon as I sweep, the thrashers put the leaves back
where they prefer them,
millipedes scattered, earwigs
        applying their calipers to gravity.
I leave a minute and the red skink enters my chair,
        an articulated sunset drawn down from the trees.
I sit only to be an Indy of flies,
        a galaxy famous only to oneself.

The minute depth was invented things began falling,
        blue light in the ocean,
the ideas of who we were, sky into the skin of book pages,
        whispers heavier than rain.
Around me the raw material, heat-induced, slippery,
        the mapping gnats, the dry and polished swallows
that cleave or shatter off like electrons.
        All this is drawn silently together,
though nothing like cellophane with its sounds
of electricity's sophisticated wrecks,
        nothing like magnets' spinning and clicking little dogs.

ONE OR MORE

Starting with greyblue-grey like East-Southeast,
      moisture made Tuesday out of ants on my white chair,
sun behind a loon and five mergansers.
Last night I held a stem that grew in my hand by adding water.
I demonstrated waxwings for Frances,
how they flew close together, each finger one or more,
      into the pear, into the pine tree,
Running Bowlines between, and Turk's Heads
and double Matthew Walkers, how they flashed like olives.
Then the difficult began:
      the material boathouse, the double birds with names
and shadows distilling forms, the two white boats like shaved
clouds that slowed and waved as *Betsy* passed *Distraction*.

I THINK SEIZURES

Passing under fan blades with the light behind,
  I think seizures and the writ of knives.
We have just begun to discovery the subsequent
and synchronous conditions,
   the arising of mushrooms after a downpour
or bright lights between billboards or a row of oaks,
   eyes rolling up, counterweighted like porcelain dolls
which, in another instance, could be ecstasy,
the impression of the odor of burnt cork and almonds.

   A little faster, little slower on the rheostat and anyone
might shudder as orioles passed into the cerebellum,
and for those moments live sporadically on wings.

WHIM OF THE MINUTE

They matter, but not for long.
Each second clicked to attention by a charged arrow
       pointing to doors that will not open though we wait.
The hour is philanthropic, the minute a miser,
concealing the otherwise least uppermost
erotic serenity of convinced societies,
       caused merely to open their eyes momentarily.

Its very tail makes a river of the fox,
       raccoon a sleeping creek in the leafed trees, a trickle
in the worms of measured pleasure,
all eating their pasts.

Second is the whim of minute that exchanges space
for candles. S was mentioned as the living river,
C was death,
       body-curl of the life-threatening.
When duration was certain, each cabin was given a boat,
       light blue to match the weather.
I cannot even remember, were the flowers near the house
white or yellow in the afterlife,
       what crisp lilies traveled within minutes of the alphabet.

THE HEAT ENGINE

In the struggle at the juncture of wills
      like math and temperature,
we cannot forget who wins, tornadoes or calm.
The effects of dispositions are not obedient to virtue
      but versions that butter the facts to their liking.
So in the family history, the spider webs
finally pull down the house,
the forger crushes old ink out of oak galls and draws
Tiepolo's deities
      draped in towels and seated on storm clouds.

The winds are not yet whistling, but learning.
      They whoosh especially well through the *ilex*
where a warn and a beckon are the same sound.

When the heat engine quits off starboard, we drift.
History's rewritten again today,
      Give and take, Take and take.
And the permutations, like giving to the living and the dead alike,
like love, like flowers.
And to the watery hopes creation is,
welcoming things that come to us breezily soft and rubber-legged,
then harden in this world.

TOUCH AND GO

One gull touches down.
A moth takes its place, rising like a second thought.

Reality is both created and displayed.

Shore breaks, on breaking,
        become amphipods and crabs, scattering
to sawgrass.
        Take and give
like the pass it on notes in school.

Little can resist this touch and go,
        this plenty for us.
But the gods have never been happy, always
coming to earth, butting in,
        to see if their pictures are still above the mantle,
their carvings stuck in the archways,
        if we saved their threatening letters,
their lies about life.

MEANWHILE

Afraid is making comebacks in the hills.
       Dark in the corners, dark upstairs
where my window, unrivered from the wind
       is my sane partner though its dead calm
grieves me.

Bees on tinfoil is the river from here
       and silk on sunset.
The Instamatic starts from the margins
       in creative ways, daylight unoffended at the bite.

Meanwhile

I am surrounded by flush left and ligatures.
       The two-pointed moon shifts reasons.
I argue with my hands as if they were airports
       waving at arrivals, sad at departures.
I know there are no dead in our estimation
       even the cities of headstones
their eyes all open as reassurance
are only half-sleepers and the paralyzed awake.

I know rock will succeed us. We will not blink
       in the face of no function
but look toward, or from what, we will forget.

BETTER ALREADY

Often overnight it happens
in answer to the hopes of moving beyond the feverish
      and the stupefying map of entrails and skin
the doctor expressing his preferences
welcoming the secret of freedom from the haunts
of endless anomalies
      anxious climates where the dim become livid
then survive
      I still have the limpets brought from Lime Kiln
chitons like sulfa ocean stones zebras streaked with quartz
whose layers of acquiescence are souvenirs
of the vast unrelenting like nines into threes into nines
      my own prescription cherished by my tribe of one
I have incised the dram glass with file lines
I have marked the place where I left off
      with my overdue bill from the ISP and the feeling
left over from the dream of enigmatic wisdom
      I hold them They relent
By morning I can be cured

Under Orion

UNDER ORION

In sweaters, under Orion and the hunt,
it is hard to remember suns are magnetic
and light is paired rails pleading for attention.
I am imagining the dense strangling matwork
of roots below the little grove of magnolia,
oak and rabbit blueberry. Frances is reading Illinois.
About us birds with short notes like dog names,
one or two syllables, something unmistakable.
The effete breeds of Westminster are lost
with their long titles. No one can call them. No bird.
They will not come. Under the roots a voice like a geode,
a beauty encased in itself lying in the earth.
We had lain down as if comfort and necessity were calling.
Oak leaves clicked on the deck. We listened like stalkers.
The planet had a heart.

THE RABBIT SOPRANO

Fear has a voice I had not expected, even from the mute.
For terror it was worse.
When I arrived she was wild-eyed, wet from their mouths,
moon-colored, feet helpless.
I heard it once long before the Irish opera using child sopranos
as woodland animals
or the Andover arts frameworks for teaching children to sing
on pitch with appropriate dynamics
the song "Mr. McGregor," or one Terese Rabbit, soprano,
now performing in Georgia,
my white Flemish Giant slipped through the pickets
without my knowing and was found by dogs.
Such human terrifying notes no known soprano hits,
mortal shrieks no composer uses,
piercing walls, urgency passing through masonry and time.

THE AGE

It was the age. People were getting messages
how to adapt, but they were old messages,
news crossing the ocean on cables, on a steaming raft,
the sky wide open but silent.
Like the out of phase patent on a petrol horse,
a tractor shaped like Dobbin down to the blinders.
The end of one thing leaves its metaphors,
no more gas derived from coal, no whalebone
after steel in m'lady's understructure.
The book in the TV news persists, the candle
still in the desk lamp. And we still have fire with its appetite,
water entering houses like night air up from the creek,
extinguishing nothing, with no comparison and nothing
to improve. The simplest landscape is one straight line.
A touch of brush and a man appears with fire arms,
ocher strikes vermillion, a horse and its enemy,
the future.

LAST ACCOMPLISHMENT

The ultimate questions are cul de sacs within which
we are double parked and out of quarters.
Below the osprey, nervousness conveyed by the water
above the mullet, aspiration in the red top hedge,
a nest of horse hair, twigs, and plastic bags.
Aquinas quoting Job repeats "my skin
will resurround me." So much do we love these bodies,
even if they were something so low as to be
abandoned by water. And what else is there
but an arrogance from the same cause, a notion
of particles each imperfect but superb, all of the elderly
interchangeable in the single hard face we are headed for.

SLEEVES RINGING

The pea coat with its hollow arms hangs dead on a brass hook,
starting a catacomb in the hall.
From elsewhere a rattle in the Coldspot door rings like milk
bottles in their wire holders,
all gone forever but in people trying to make a case for something—
form in poetry, god in the bread,
the old unchanging— all confirmed in the thirsty nervousness of sleep.
Voices in the mountains of sonar
in osillography may be the heart talking, or the migrating whales
of forgiveness, grey and transitory,
steaming south past Cape Flattery. I am only making a case for tornadoes
talking too fast for understanding,
thunder mumbling names, pointing to the blood, to the empty arms,
sleeves ringing like alive.

TRICHOEPITHELIOMA

I come across "tumor" and something from last night
stirs like a lungfish,
and something like Italy from Naples to Sorrento
wiggles on the cliffs
in a movie, like balloons hovering musically above,
the rude neutrinos
blanched and swollen twice their size, and giddy
from the sun.
Then a flounder starts to come unglued like a label
and moves along the coast,
scoots off like a ruffle, the shape of the alarm
that wakes me.
Again I remember the solid world seeing the smallest thing.
I look at my stitches like a comb.

ONE SO EXOTIC

The world I'm aware of implies one
many times larger
one that exists in no illustrated guidebooks
One so exotic
a gnat could be Pluto since nature is showing us
only what it must
and we are making up the rest from the view
through a mail slot
a one-way eye in the door of the Comfort Inn

Startled minnows sound like a fling of gravel
pea not potato
jacks behind them flashing like the flea market's
table of scissors and knives
I think they are menhaden I think they are coins
never identified
A woman calls in to report with the power out
she saw what she thought
was the Aurora for the first time reaching Cleveland

AVIS

No less ferocious than Lorenz wanting to be a goose,
is the belief in not enough to go around,
as I believe in plenty and France when I get there
and not before, and not because
of some fey arabesques in plaster or a gold mirror's
widening coy smiles.
I belive the ocean loves me for my solid placidity.
It comforts me up to my arched neck.
I love it for telepathy as it sends goosebumps from Nice
and the grey feathered evenings,
the melodious voices of Algerians wanting to trade shoes
when we finished swimming.
Need is a government following the first thing moving,
envy its ministers, its gods toxic.
All that is unnecessary. Plenty would fly to us
even had we been Belgian, or Cygnus Olor, a mute swan
or a rented car.

INSTRUCTIONS

We see the dark we lie down in by feeling.
The eye leaps from the hand.
A shadow stops suddenly, unlikely for shadows.
A bird has landed above me.
In the wind, gasoline and coconut mean neighbors
with inlaws have come for the weekend
followed by shouting and blasphemy .

On the bright side a bird
is doing variations on a comb and tissue paper.
Before I see it I stare
into the distance and read the island as a line
of instructive dignity,
today Emerson, yesterday Muir and Vico.
I do as they say.
I cut loose a beetle from a spiderless web
while its brethren sing to my ears.
I write more than the senses can deliver,
the croon of the island, the letter of the law.

READY FOR BLUEBIRDS

I couldn't do anything about the too-close trees
but put up the houses in the widest space oakwise,
the ones with the copper rings in the entry and no perch
as suggested for just such thrushes, blue and rust-chested,
with the young birds speckled as far as Nicaragua.
They have been ignored four years, all the while sun
traveled up and down on its wires, doves lamented
their pea brains to the ferns and spirea, deck chairs cuddled
with their X & Y webbing turned so as not to seem staring
or a trap. Ocean was a film. Windows aquaria. Fringe of spartina
the first ahoy. So dressed in welcome it looked like a
holy coast. While I wait my hands are ringing, my teeth
expectantly adjusting in bone.

IMAGINATIVE HABITS

Someone poses before concrete. Two rough complexions.
They will not mix, nor will the oak after 30 years
stop shouldering the house. It just gets worse.
So speaks history and future with the same face,
bones and leaves named for what they look like,
imaginative habits, a heart afraid for itself,
what we least easily believe.
In the right-handed universe—this one—are remnants of another
or some letters from one to come.
The lightning whelk and several writers I know
are the ends or the emissaries.
I remember as a child the flour sifter.
With it I made moons on the counter and waxed paper.
I used it with either hand and was a ghost.
I stood softly before the planets as one of them.

ONE WORLD APPEARING AS TWO

Individual ruin is inevitable,
but meanwhile take your hand's enchantments
while they last.
The indicative finger dictates speech and points
to the days remaining and leads the band.
I had gone to the dock at Friday Harbor
for a boat to locate whales
which were fingers from a myth.
While I waited a glass tank held a octopus
to my palm and when I asked for my experience
the last ticket sold.
So I went instead to the blond-headed meadow
above the cliffs, the wind's many fingers
parting and combing, a giant's hand
toying with its hair.
One description tells history, another denies it.
In another, a silver ring marries the moon
to the moist sky, the thirst of the simple chemistries
of the muscle to its musical nerves,
dexterous, apterous, alive.

THE SPEED OF LIGHT

Despite its reputation that nothing exceed it,
it lingers on the pond,
leaves only reluctantly from the nervous,
silvery cottonwoods
gathered at the edge like a camping family.
But, once vanished,
it stays out all night in another galaxy
leaving breadcrumbs to get back.
That's nothing.
I can be here one minute where the strings
of the driveway
are purposely united during daylight,
then to Jupiter and back
where one harebell starts the yard in its frenzy
of reexplaining.
What takes its place appears lovingly
like caressing a pet,
a Lab starting black and ending golden
as we float in our bodies
of blood and rubble so rich we'll hardly miss it,
a song at the end instead of a period